Copyright © 2025 by JT Publishing

ISBN: 979-8-9998110-0-4

All rights reserved. No part of this publication may be reproduced, or transmitted in any form or by any means, including photocopying, recording, or other electronic or mechanical methods, without the prior written permission of the publisher.

Published by: JT Publishing

Printed in the United States of America

SET FREE 2 LIVE

MY JOURNEY THROUGH POSTPARTUM DEPRESSION AND ANXIETY

THERESA M. THOMAS

This book is dedicated to God, Jesus, and the Holy Spirit. My husband James, daughters, Alexis and Nasiya, my mother, Nan and bonus mom, Bernice.

In remembrance of my dad Eugene Stevenson.

TABLE OF CONTENTS

Prologue

I share this journey not only for women navigating postpartum depression, but for anyone who has experienced the weight of **depression or anxiety** in their lifetime. Even as I began writing this book, I found myself facing another personal battle—this time, sparked by a health scare that reawakened old fears. That's the thing about depression: it doesn't always come with a warning. It can sneak in quietly, catching us off guard.

Through every chapter of my life—from escaping an abusive marriage, to struggling with infertility, to surviving postpartum depression—**God has carried me**. Looking back, I can clearly see His hand guiding every season, even the painful ones. It hasn't always been easy, but it has always been **on purpose** and in **His timing**.

Writing this book has required me to revisit some of the darkest places I've ever been. I've even returned to the very neighborhood where my postpartum journey began—a place filled with memories I couldn't ignore, and stories I now feel called to share.

I never imagined postpartum depression would be part of my story. In fact, I didn't even know what it truly was. Now, I know better. And I believe more people need to know better too. Postpartum depression is real. It's serious. And it should never be dismissed or minimized.

My hope is that this book helps raise awareness, open dialogue, and offer comfort to those who are suffering silently. Far too many women endure postpartum depression without the support they need—sometimes feeling ashamed, isolated, or spiritually conflicted.

For a long time, I resisted taking medication. As a Christian, I thought it meant I wasn't trusting God enough. But I've come to understand that faith and treatment can coexist. **God can work through prayer *and* prescription.** He began healing me the moment I surrendered, not just to Him, but to the help He was sending my way.

I went 16 years without needing medication again. Then, a new storm hit, and once again, medication helped me find steady ground. And God was still with me.

So wherever you are today, in the joy of new motherhood, in the fog of depression, or standing beside someone who is hurting—I pray this story encourages you. I pray it gives you faith, strength, and hope to trust that **God is not only with you in the storm... He is carrying you through it.**

You are not alone.

And you don't have to stay in the dark.

CHAPTER 1

UNUSUAL LOVE

*He who finds a wife finds a good thing and obtains favor
from the Lord.*

— PROVERBS 18:22

I t all began in 1998 when I was stationed at Fort Campbell,
Kentucky. By then, I had been in the Army for four years,
far longer than I ever intended. Truthfully, I had only
joined to escape my abusive husband. What I didn't know at
the time was that it was all a divine setup, not orchestrated by
me, but by fate, to lead me to the love of my life.

After enduring a four-year abusive marriage, the last thing
I wanted was another serious relationship. While stationed at
Fort Campbell, I dated occasionally, but trust was something I
no longer had in men. I had made a vow: no man would ever
lay hands on me again. From that marriage, I had one child,
my oldest daughter, Alexis. I often feared that her father would
harm her too, and I knew I had to make a move.

Even my mother-in-law at the time urged me to leave. But
fear gripped me. Where would I go? I hadn't told my parents
what was happening. To quietly escape, I joined the military,
ironically, at my husband's suggestion. He thought it would

be a way for me to make money while he traveled. But I had a different plan. This was my ticket out. I sent Alexis to live with my mom and left for Army basic training.

My first duty station was Fort Hood, Texas. That's where I finally filed for divorce. Alexis' father never responded or signed the papers, so the divorce was granted uncontested. My next station was Fort Campbell, Kentucky, much closer to my hometown of Nashville, Tennessee. While there, Alexis' father reached out, wanting to see her. By then, she was four years old and hadn't seen him in over two years.

Reluctantly, I agreed, but on my terms. We met at the mall, and he brought his girlfriend. Alexis had fun with her father, and seeing her happy made me drop my guard. I even allowed them to come back to the house for more time together. Before leaving, he promised her he'd return the next morning.

The next day, Alexis sat by the window, eyes full of hope. Hours passed, but he never came. "When is my daddy coming?" she asked, her voice full of innocence and hurt.

My heart shattered. I regretted letting him re-enter her life, only to disappoint her again. I vowed that I would never allow him to hurt her like that again. We moved on, and we didn't hear from him again until Alexis turned eighteen.

In the military, my role was mostly administrative. Part of my duties involved delivering documents to higher-ranking personnel for approvals. During those trips, I often ran into Sergeant Thomas. He was always around, but I never paid much attention to him. At that time, I had been divorced for six years and wasn't remotely interested in dating.

One day, out of the blue, Sergeant Thomas handed me a slip of paper—his phone number. "Call me," he said with a confident smile.

Let me be honest: He was not my type. Shorter than six feet, wore thick glasses, and drove a sky-blue hooptie. Yes, a full-on hooptie. I wasn't impressed. I tucked his number into my folder and forgot about it.

Months passed. I was preparing to attend training at Fort Jackson, South Carolina, to qualify for Staff Sergeant. It was a three-month course, and I looked forward to the change of pace.

My roommate at the course was Sgt. Hayes, a kind, God-fearing woman. We got along well. Training was tough—early mornings at 4 a.m. and long days, but weekends were ours to relax. One weekend, I met a man at the school who caught my attention. We hung out a few times, but I later learned he was married. Though I liked him, I knew that was a red flag. I chose to walk away, believing God was telling me, "This is not for you."

One evening while digging through my belongings, I found that forgotten slip of paper—Sergeant Thomas' number. How did this get here? I could've sworn I threw it away.

I told Sgt. Hayes, and she laughed. "Girl, you might as well call him."

So I did.

To my surprise, he remembered me. What started as a quick call turned into hours of conversation. We clicked. The more we spoke, the more I found myself calling him.

Later, Hayes mentioned she'd been stationed with him in Germany. Coincidence? I didn't think so. I began to wonder if this was divine intervention.

When I returned from training, James and I decided to meet. We had dinner, watched TV, and talked into the night. I felt safe, something I hadn't felt in a long time. Despite his "hooptie" and those glasses, I found myself genuinely liking him.

We grew close, but then came the unexpected: new orders. I was being sent to Korea; James was headed to Colorado. This was before FaceTime and texting—just emails and handwritten letters. We weren't sure a long-distance relationship would work, so we decided to stay friends.

Even after James left, we kept in touch. And when I deployed to Korea, our connection remained strong. Distance only made our bond stronger. Eventually, we made a decision: When I returned home for mid-tour leave, we'd get married.

During my layover in Denver en route to Nashville, James met me at the gate—back when airport security still allowed it. He greeted me with a teddy bear and a warm smile. We barely had time to talk. I didn't know it then, but hidden beneath the bear's ribbon was an engagement ring. I boarded the plane unaware I had just been proposed to.

It wasn't until I sat down and examined the bear that I saw it. A ring. I was stunned, and deeply touched.

About a week later, Alexis and I flew to Colorado. We stayed at James' one-bedroom apartment. Because we weren't married, and out of respect for Alexis, we didn't sleep in the same room. She was around seven or eight at the time and initially resistant to the idea of me getting remarried. But with time, she came around.

On June 30, 2000—James' birthday—we got married at the courthouse in Denver. No big ceremony. Just a quiet, meaningful exchange of vows.

I returned to Nashville for the remainder of my leave, and soon after, I flew back to Korea to finish my tour. No honeymoon. No newlywed glow. Just service, duty, and love stretched across miles.

Seven months later, I returned to the States. James, Alexis, and I moved to Colorado Springs to begin our life together.

It wasn't without challenges. Alexis had to adjust to having a new father figure, but James stepped in with love, patience, and commitment. Eventually, he officially adopted her, and she took his last name.

As our marriage blossomed, I felt incredibly blessed. But there was still one thing missing.

James wanted a child of his own—a legacy, a namesake. And I knew in my heart, it was something we both deeply desired.

Chapter 2

Trials and Tribulations

These things I have spoken to you, that in me you may have peace.
In the world you will have tribulation; but be of good cheer, I have overcome the world.
— John 16:33

Life at Fort Carson, Colorado, was beginning to feel like home. Alexis had settled into her new school, and for the first time in a while, there was a sense of calm in our household. Within a year of our marriage, I found out I was pregnant.

We were overjoyed. We hadn't been actively trying—we had simply placed our faith in God, trusting that He would choose the right time. When I shared the news with James, he was overwhelmed with happiness. He had always wanted a child of his own, and now that dream was finally within reach.

I started preparing right away, excitedly buying maternity clothes and daydreaming about our future. But something felt off—I was already swelling earlier than expected. My mother, who was equally ecstatic about the new addition to our family, gifted us a stunning baby furniture set. I knew it cost her a fortune, but she didn't hesitate—she was just as ready to welcome a new grandchild.

It felt like everything was falling into place.

Until it wasn't.

Despite our excitement, there were tensions in our marriage. James struggled to express his emotions, and I had difficulty letting things go. When we argued, he'd often leave and stay gone for hours, or sometimes even days, without speaking to me. These periods of silence left me confused, insecure, and emotionally exhausted. Though he'd eventually return with an apology, the emotional damage lingered.

One night, I got up to use the bathroom and noticed spotting. My heart sank. "This can't be right," I whispered to myself. Panic crept in. I woke James and told him we needed to get to the hospital.

At the ER, the technician performed an ultrasound. The silence in the room was deafening. Though the scan lasted only about 30 minutes, it felt like an eternity. When the doctor returned, I saw the look on her face and knew the news wasn't good.

"We couldn't find a fetus," she said softly.

I was stunned. "What do you mean you can't find a fetus? What have I been carrying all this time?"

James walked in just as I was grappling with the news. I looked at him, tears forming in my eyes. "They said there's no baby."

The doctor explained that I was experiencing a miscarriage.

"No. No, this isn't happening to me," I cried out, my voice trembling with disbelief and anguish. I broke down, sobbing uncontrollably. James held me as I cried in the hospital room, but the pain was unimaginable.

I called my mom hysterically crying. I kept thinking to myself what I did wrong. Why is this happening to me?

Back home, I stayed curled up in my husband's arms, still clinging to the faint hope that the doctors were wrong. I kept wishing to feel something move inside me—some sign of life. I had read stories of women who spotted during pregnancy and still had healthy babies.

The next day, still in denial, we saw another doctor. She confirmed that while there had been a sac and an umbilical cord, the fetus had never developed. It was a condition known as a blighted ovum. My body had gone through the motions of pregnancy without carrying a baby.

That evening, we just held each other and cried. I noticed James was crying too. It was the first time I had ever seen him cry.

Soon, nature began to take its course. The physical pain was excruciating—far worse than any menstrual cramps I had ever experienced. I was doubled over, unable to do anything but cry. When the sac finally passed, I could hardly process the grief. I was completely devastated.

For months, I blamed myself. I questioned everything— what I ate, how much I rested, whether I had lifted something too heavy. Guilt consumed me. I couldn't stop wondering, "What did I do wrong?"

In desperation, I met with a military chaplain. He was compassionate and prayerful. He reassured me that some things are simply beyond our control and that this loss wasn't my fault. He suggested that I write a letter to the baby. Though I didn't know the gender, I felt in my heart that it was a girl. I wrote her a heartfelt letter and tucked it away in my Bible, where it remains to this day. Writing that letter brought a small sense of peace.

In an effort to lift my spirits, James planned a trip to Las Vegas for our anniversary. He hoped that a change of scenery would help, and I did my best to enjoy it. We went to a show and relaxed by the pool, but the summer heat was overwhelming, and the weight of my grief followed me everywhere. I smiled, but it was forced. Nothing could fill the void.

Five months later, I missed another period. I took a test—it was positive. Hope flickered in my heart, only to be extinguished days later by another miscarriage. This one came and went so quickly, I barely had time to process it.

Still, James and I didn't give up. We tried again and again, but nothing happened. A year passed, and I was now 35. I found myself praying, "Lord, I don't want to be Sarah, having a baby in my old age!"

We decided to see a fertility specialist. I underwent countless tests—blood work, ultrasounds, and dye studies to check for blockages. James had his sperm count tested (he was a little embarrassed, but relieved when everything came back normal). Despite all the testing, no one could explain why we weren't getting pregnant.

Then, life interrupted again.

In 2000, James was put on standby to deploy to Kuwait. We had planned a family trip to Disney World but had to cancel it. I was also up for re-enlistment. With both of us potentially deploying and Alexis at home, I had to make a choice. I chose not to re-enlist. I received an Honorable Discharge and transferred to the Army Reserves.

By 2002, James had deployed to Kuwait, and my unit was sent to Iraq. The separation was difficult. I clung to every letter, every phone call. To help with the loneliness, Alexis and I adopted a little Lhasa Apso puppy and named him Teddy.

One winter, we got snowed in during a blizzard in Colorado. Cabin fever set in quickly, and Alexis and I shoveled ourselves out with help from kind neighbors. Life was hard, but we got through it together.

After seven long months, James returned home. He put in for retirement, and it was approved. He flew back on a massive military transport and officially retired from the Army.

We resumed our efforts to conceive but still had no success. That's when our doctor recommended in vitro fertilization (IVF).

Because we were both in the military, we qualified for discounted IVF treatment at Walter Reed Medical Center in Washington, D.C. We packed up our things and made the trip from Georgia, where we had recently relocated. While we were there, we took time to sightsee with Alexis, now almost 13.

At the orientation, they explained the IVF process in detail. We watched a video, and when they mentioned sperm collection, I chuckled, thinking, "My husband is not going to want to do this again." We met with a counselor and put down a $350 deposit.

But there was a complication. Someone had to stay in D.C. with me for the duration of the treatment—up to a month. James couldn't leave Alexis, and my mom couldn't take off work. I asked my best friend Catherine, but her time off wasn't guaranteed.

I felt stuck. I cried out to God: "Lord, if there's any other way, please bless us."

A month later, I missed my period.

At first, I ignored it. I didn't want to get my hopes up again. But when the days kept passing, I quietly took a pregnancy test.

Positive.

I didn't tell James right away. I wanted to be sure. On Mother's Day, we went out to eat near the mall. While waiting for a table, I couldn't hold it in any longer. I told James and Alexis, "There's a strong possibility I'm pregnant."

James looked at me, surprised and cautious. We had been through so much heartbreak. I assured him I had a doctor's appointment the next day to confirm it.

The next day, the doctor confirmed what we'd been praying for—pregnant!

Joy and fear battled within me. We had been here before. But when we heard the heartbeat and saw the ultrasound, we knew it was real.

God had answered our prayers.

We canceled the IVF process, and Walter Reed refunded every penny. After years of heartbreak and waiting, we were finally going to have a baby.

CHAPTER 3

THE BUNDLE OF JOY

Every good gift and every perfect gift is from above,
And comes down from the Father of lights
With whom there is no variation or shadow of turning
— JAMES 1:17

A t three months pregnant, I was still serving in the Army Reserves and had to report to Fort Gordon—in Augusta, Georgia. This was the first time in my military career that I was pregnant while actively serving. It felt special in a way, especially when I joined the physical training sessions specifically designated for pregnant soldiers.

Still, I couldn't shake my fear. After everything we had endured—multiple miscarriages, years of waiting, the emotional rollercoaster—I was overly cautious, terrified that something might go wrong. I tried my best to avoid stress, but being in the military made that nearly impossible, especially under demanding leadership.

At home, I had a fetal Doppler monitor so I could listen to the baby's heartbeat. I checked it religiously, finding comfort each time I heard that steady rhythm. Then, one day, I heard nothing.

Panic set in immediately. What if my baby isn't breathing? What if something is wrong?

I had an appointment scheduled in a few days, but the wait was agonizing. When the time finally came, I sat nervously on the exam table, bracing myself for the worst. As soon as the monitor touched my belly, a strong, steady heartbeat filled the room.

Relief washed over me. My baby was okay.

A few weeks later, we had our 3D ultrasound to find out the baby's gender. James was hoping for a boy, but as the image formed on the screen, the technician smiled and said, "It's a girl!"

James tried to hide his slight disappointment, but I didn't mind. All I wanted was a healthy baby. That was my prayer every day.

As my pregnancy progressed, the military environment became increasingly toxic. My Sergeant Major had a habit of nitpicking and micro-managing. If someone returned from lunch even one minute late or didn't stand at attention fast enough during formation, it became a big issue. For some reason, it felt personal—as if she had it out for me.

One afternoon, after lunch with James, I returned to base just a few minutes late. I was immediately called into the office. My Sergeant Major and the Commander sat across from me with stern expressions.

"Why were you late?" she asked sharply.

I explained, but the embarrassment and stress lingered. It felt like all the years I had poured into my military service didn't count for anything.

That evening, I talked to James. He had already retired from the military and was still receiving pay from his accumulated leave. Between that and his upcoming retirement check, we were financially secure.

"Maybe it's time to step away," he said.

I prayed and thought long and hard. I had served in the military 11 years. No job, no matter how much I valued it, was worth risking my health or my baby's well-being.

So, I made the decision.

I submitted my paperwork for separation due to pregnancy.

And just like that, my military career came to an end.

By the time I was around seven months pregnant, we decided to move closer to family in the Atlanta area. This meant Alexis had to change schools again. But being a military child, she had grown used to these transitions.

We settled in Henry County, in Hampton, Georgia. It felt like the perfect location—not too far from my hometown of Nashville, Tennessee, and not too far from James' family in Florida.

At her new school, Alexis made the basketball team. She loved playing and adjusted well with her teammates. She was now a teenager, and with that came the typical attitude and growing pains. One day, before a scheduled game, she left the house without our permission. We had no idea where she went.

I was trying to manage my stress for the baby's sake, but this incident pushed me to my limit. When she came back home with her friends, I calmly asked where she had been.

When I realized she hadn't asked for permission, James and I decided to punish her by not allowing her to play in the game. She was furious. She stormed upstairs, and moments later we heard a loud crash—shattering glass. I raced up the stairs, terrified. To my relief, there was no blood—just a broken window.

Once she calmed down, we had a heart-to-heart conversation. She understood what she had done wrong, and slowly, we moved forward.

James began looking for work. He applied for government jobs but had no luck. Eventually, he found a job at a battery packaging factory, working night shifts. Meanwhile, I was eight months pregnant and not working at all. It didn't make sense to start a job only to go on maternity leave shortly after.

My belly grew larger, and our baby girl was active—kicking constantly and reminding me of her strength. By now, I was 38 years old. Never in a million years did I think I'd be having a baby at this age.

December 2005 arrived. I was officially nine months pregnant.

The excitement built with every passing day. Would this be another New Year's Eve baby? I was scheduled for a C-section on January 11, but I knew babies had their own plans. Like most pregnant women, I had my share of false alarms. Each time I rushed to the hospital, only to be sent back home. I was ready, physically and emotionally, to meet my little one.

Then, on January 9, I had a routine doctor's appointment.

As soon as my doctor examined me, she frowned. "How are you feeling?"

"I've had some pain," I admitted, "but nothing too serious."

She shook her head. "It's time. Head straight to the hospital."

I blinked in disbelief. "Right now?"

"Yes," she nodded. "This baby is ready to come out."

Panic set in. James was at work. Alexis was in school. I hadn't even packed my hospital bag.

I called James immediately. He rushed home, packed my things, and met me at the hospital. Thankfully, my cousin, who had been staying with us, picked Alexis up from school.

As I sat in my hospital room, reality sank in. I was finally going to meet my miracle baby.

James arrived, and we waited. They gave me the epidural, and I laid there, emotions swirling.

At around 9:00 p.m., the nurses came in to prep me for surgery.

This wasn't my first C-section, so I knew the process. But for James, it was all new. I wondered how he'd handle it.

At 10:15 p.m., the doctor made the incision. I felt the familiar tugging. A few seconds passed in silence. Then—finally—a strong, loud cry.

She was here.

We had already chosen her name: **Nasiya**, which means "miracle from God."

Tears streamed down my face.
She was our miracle.
Life couldn't be better.
Or so we thought.

CHAPTER 4

THE STORM

When you pass through the waters
I will be with you; and through the rivers,
They shall not overflow you.
When you walk through the fire you shall not be burned
Nor shall the flame scorch you.
— ISAIAH 43:2

Bringing Nasiya home was a moment of pure joy. She was beautiful, precious, and everything we had prayed for. I nursed her, held her close, and bonded with her in those first few weeks. Her big sister, Alexis, adored her and was always eager to help. It felt like we had finally stepped into the season of answered prayers. Life felt complete.

Then, just three weeks after her birth, James came home from work early, his face unusually serious.

"I got fired," he said flatly.

I blinked in disbelief. "Fired?"

My heart sank. We had a newborn, no current income from my side, and though we still had James's military retirement check and some savings, the thought of losing our primary income source threw me into a panic. How would we pay our bills? What about diapers, formula, or emergencies? I couldn't understand why he seemed so calm.

James tried to reassure me, brushing it off as a blessing in disguise. He hadn't liked the job much anyway. But I couldn't feel what he felt. I was overwhelmed by fear.

Around that same time, I got a phone call from my mother in Nashville. She sounded terrible, her voice weak and strained.

"I think I've come down with something bad," she said. "And your grandmother isn't doing well either."

The weight of her words hit hard. My mother had always been the caregiver in our family. If she couldn't care for herself or my grandmother, then things were worse than she was letting on.

With little hesitation, I packed up the baby and drove nearly five hours to Nashville. It was my first time traveling that distance with a newborn. While I should have been excited to introduce my baby to my mom and grandma, something inside me felt heavy. I was exhausted in ways I couldn't explain. Still, I pushed forward.

When we arrived, my fears were confirmed. My mother looked sickly and pale. She barely had the energy to sit up and couldn't even hold her new granddaughter. My grandmother wasn't doing well either. Without any other options, I became the one responsible for everyone.

I was cooking, cleaning, nursing a newborn, and trying to care for two sick adults—all while barely sleeping. It quickly became too much, but I didn't know how to say so.

One afternoon, I met my best friend Catherine for lunch in Nashville. This was her first time meeting Nasiya. I tried to put on a brave face, but Catherine knew me too well. She immediately noticed the dark circles under my eyes and my forced smile. I was usually bubbly and full of laughter, but not this time.

"Are you okay?" she asked gently.

I nodded, brushing it off. "Just tired."

After lunch, we took a stroll through the park. I pushed the stroller, trying to soak in the fresh air, but I felt disconnected—from my baby, from my friend, from myself. I couldn't shake the feeling that something was very wrong. I had prayed for this baby for years. I had gone through so much to bring her into the world. Why did I feel so numb?

Things didn't improve at my mom's house. I started having terrible insomnia. My thoughts were constantly racing. Even when I closed my eyes, my mind wouldn't shut off. I blamed it on exhaustion and hormones. But deep down, I knew it was more than that.

After five days, my mom started feeling a little better, so I packed us up and returned home. But the darkness followed me.

James and I were still figuring things out financially, and the stress weighed heavily on our relationship. We began arguing more. I became irritable and withdrawn. Every little thing he did annoyed me. The sound of the baby crying made my skin crawl.

Worst of all, I began feeling disconnected from Nasiya. I loved her, but I didn't feel like I was bonding. Nursing became a chore. Her cries made me anxious. I dreaded being alone with her, not because I feared her, but because I feared my thoughts.

One day, as I rocked her in my arms, a horrifying thought flashed through my mind: *Throw her out the window.*

I gasped, my entire body going still. Where did that come from? That's not me. I would never hurt my child!

Would I?

That moment shook me to my core. I started crying more. Sometimes I'd cry for hours without knowing why. Nothing brought relief—not prayer, not church, not even time.

At my postpartum check-up, I finally opened up. "I can't stop crying," I confessed. "I feel like I'm losing my mind."

The doctor nodded slowly. "It sounds like postpartum depression," she said. "I recommend seeing a psychiatrist."

The idea terrified me. I wasn't crazy. I wasn't like the women on the news who harmed their babies. But I went. The psychiatrist asked a list of questions, then referred me to a counselor and prescribed medication. I had never taken medication for my mental health before. I was hesitant. I feared becoming dependent.

Still, I went to the counselor for three sessions. But I didn't feel better. I wasn't eating. I was losing weight fast. I gave up breastfeeding altogether. James tried to help, but he didn't know what to do.

We took a trip to visit his uncle in South Carolina and went to church with them. After the service, I had a panic attack in the parking lot. I broke down crying. Sherrie, his uncle's wife, talked to me gently.

"You need to take the medicine," she said. "There's no shame in getting help."

Back at our home, I began searching online and found a postpartum support group. I called and spoke to a woman who had been through it. Hearing her voice and knowing she understood gave me hope, but I still couldn't bring myself to take the medication.

My family from Nashville came to visit—my father, Bernice (my bonus mother), my little sister, and niece. I tried to keep it together, but the cracks were showing. I confided a little in Bernice. She prayed over me, but I could tell she didn't fully realize how bad things were.

One Sunday, we all went to church. I expected peace—church was usually my safe space. But halfway through the service, panic took over. I turned to Bernice in tears.

"Something is wrong," I whispered. "I'm not okay."

We walked out to the parking lot, and I let everything pour out: I couldn't sleep or eat. I felt disconnected from my baby. I had terrifying thoughts. I was scared.

She listened carefully and then handed me a number. "Call her," she said. "She's someone I know that suffered from the same thing you are going through."

I promised I would.

Even with support and prayers, one question haunted me: **Will I ever get better?**

CHAPTER 5

LOSING MY MIND

For God did not give us the spirit of fear,
but of power, and of love, and of a sound mind.
— 2 TIMOTHY 1:7

Several weeks had passed since my symptoms first began. By now, I had completely refused to take the medication the doctor had prescribed. Something inside me convinced me that it would poison my body. A woman from church had warned me about the side effects, and that was all the confirmation I needed.

So, I suffered. And things only got worse.

One night, I woke up in a panic. My heart was racing, my breathing shallow. I shook James awake, my voice trembling. "The devil is telling me I don't believe!" I cried.

James tried to calm me down, holding me close, but I couldn't shake the feeling that something was tormenting me. Another night, it happened again. This time, I jumped out of bed and started banging the floor with my fists. I had terrifying thoughts that I was going to die, that I was not really a believer. It felt like the enemy was whispering, "You are a sinner, and you're going to hell because you don't believe."

"Leave me alone!" I shouted, pacing from room to room, rebuking the torment in my mind. I knew my family thought I was losing it, but I didn't care.

I wasn't sleeping at all. If I closed my eyes, the thoughts would come rushing in. I started turning on the TV just to drown them out, flipping through channels until I found something to give me peace. One night, I landed on a Joyce Meyer sermon. She was teaching on *Battlefield of the Mind*. I had never been a big fan, but I was desperate. I listened, and something clicked.

It wasn't full relief, but it was something.

I started watching her every night. Then I added Creflo Dollar to my playlist. He talked about fear and panic attacks. It felt like God was trying to reach me through these messages. The Word of God gave me a small sense of peace in the chaos.

My days and nights flipped. I'd sleep during the day and stay up at night. But even then, new fears crept in—like aging. I became obsessed with how old I would be when Nasiya graduated high school. I did the math over and over. How many years did I have left?

One afternoon, Alexis and I went to the mall. All I could see were gray-haired people everywhere. It overwhelmed me. Why was this bothering me now?

"Take me to the bathroom," I whispered to Alexis. We rushed into a family restroom. I tried to breathe and calm myself down, but I couldn't. I asked her to pray with me. I'm sure she was confused, but she did it anyway. After praying and breathing together, the fear lifted, just enough to walk back out.

That night, I gave in and took the medication. But after two days, I still felt awful. So I flushed the pills down the toilet. I didn't tell anyone. I was too embarrassed.

A friend suggested herbal remedies, so I went to an herb shop. The man behind the counter gave me some supplements. They helped a little, but not enough. I was still not sleeping. I was barely functioning. Most of all, I still wasn't bonding with my baby.

I felt like a terrible mother. I didn't want to kill myself, but I didn't want to live either.

One night around 2:00 a.m., unable to sleep, I thought, *I have to get out of here.* I threw on clothes and left the house. I ran through the darkness with no destination in mind.

If I get hit by a car, maybe it will all be over.

There's a train track nearby.

Maybe I could just end it. But then, something in me said, *No.*

I went back home. James never even knew I had left.

Then the hallucinations began. I tried reading my Bible, but I couldn't concentrate. One night, the words on the page started moving. I gasped. "Am I seeing things?"

Another night, I went out on the back patio, crying out to God. "Please help me, Lord! Take this away from me! I just want to be normal again!" I wept so hard I felt like I might never stop. Suddenly, my right leg began jerking uncontrollably—up and down, up and down. I stared at it, terrified. Was God trying to get my attention?

Eventually, it stopped.

I turned on another Joyce Meyer sermon. She talked about her book *Battlefield of the Mind*. I thought, *I have to get that book.*

Someone from church suggested I get away for a little while. James booked a hotel for me nearby. At first, I thought it might help. But as I sat in the quiet, loneliness crept in. I tried to read my Bible but couldn't focus. I went to the indoor pool, hoping the water might help. It helped a little, but not enough.

Back in the room, the thoughts returned: *You're getting old. You're going to die. You won't be around for Nasiya.* I prayed in the Holy Ghost for hours, begging for relief. But still— nothing changed.

Then, I remembered the number my bonus mom Bernice gave me—Isla. I called her.

She listened. She understood. She had been through it. Everything she described mirrored what I was going through. But she took the medication. She got better. She prayed with me.

For the first time in months, I felt hope.

She told me I could call her anytime. And I did.

There were nights when I couldn't sleep, when fear would wake me up in a sweat. I'd call Isla—even at 2:00 a.m. She would answer. She'd talk with me. Pray with me. Calm me down.

I started calling her most mornings because that's when my anxiety was the worst. I often wondered, *Who was there for her when she went through this?*

No matter how many prayers were said, no matter how many encouraging words I heard, the darkness still lingered.

The thoughts still came.

And I started to wonder if this was just going to be my life now.

I felt hopeless.

Would I ever be free again?

CHAPTER 6

OUT OF PLACE

Greater is He that is in me than he that is in the world.
— 1 JOHN 4:4

By now, I was truly desperate.

One day, I went for a walk in the park by myself while James stayed home with the baby. I sat on a bench and just cried. It seemed like crying had become a daily ritual, something as regular as brushing my teeth. I didn't care who saw me—I almost hoped someone would. Maybe they'd ask if I was okay, maybe they'd sit with me, maybe they'd even pray with me. More than anything, I longed for prayer, for connection, for someone to stand in the gap and intercede when I couldn't find the words myself.

The tears wouldn't stop. "Why, God? Why is this happening to me? Why can't I just be happy again?" My thoughts spiraled as I sat there. Then, a random idea came to mind— call a church. Any church. It didn't make sense since I already belonged to a local church, but my mind was not functioning clearly. Everything felt jumbled and frantic. I pulled up a nearby church's number on my phone and called, praying someone would pick up.

No one answered.

That silence confirmed what I already felt—utterly and completely alone.

When I got home, I looked at James and said, "I think I need to go to the hospital. I don't know how much more I can take." Without hesitation, he packed up Nasiya, and we drove to the ER.

While sitting in the waiting room, I struck up a conversation with an older woman nearby. Oddly, I didn't feel panic around her. Her gentle spirit brought a calm I hadn't felt in weeks. She didn't have to say much. Her presence alone made me feel safe.

Eventually, the nurse called me back. She asked dozens of questions, and I answered as honestly as I could. When she asked if I'd had thoughts of harming myself or the baby, I nodded and whispered, "Yes."

Within twenty minutes, I was in the back of an ambulance. I didn't get to say goodbye to James or kiss Nasiya. I didn't even know where I was going. Panic rose in my chest as the ambulance drove for what felt like forever and finally pulled up to Riverwood Psychiatric Facility.

I froze.

Am I being committed? What's happening? Will I ever see my family again?

They took all of my belongings and escorted me to a room—bare, cold, unfamiliar. I sat alone, terrified and confused. "Why am I here?" I thought. "They must have made a mistake. I would never hurt my baby. I just... I just needed help."

A nurse came in and explained they were going to start me on medication. I didn't argue. I swallowed the pill and, for the first time in months, I slept. Not the restless tossing and turning I had grown used to—but real, peaceful sleep.

The next day, as night fell again, I became more aware of my surroundings. One man shuffled endlessly up and down the hall, his slippers dragging on the linoleum—shuffle, shuffle, shuffle. It was haunting. Another woman paced frantically, mumbling to herself with eyes full of fear.

I don't belong here.

Tears streamed down my face. I prayed desperately. "God, why did You bring me here?"

Then, I met a young woman who was crying uncontrollably. She had just suffered a miscarriage. My heart broke for her, and I shared my own story. We cried together. We prayed together. She asked me to stay, and so I did. We sat and talked for hours. Somehow, comforting her began to heal a part of me.

For the first time in a long while, I felt useful. I started praying with other women, listening to their pain, and offering encouragement. Maybe this was why I was here. Maybe this was part of my purpose.

By day three, I found myself speaking during group therapy. The facilitator read from the Bible and asked for reflections. Without hesitation, I shared. I spoke of faith, endurance, and God's grace. The words flowed like water, as if the Holy Spirit Himself was speaking through me.

Was it the medication? Was it divine intervention? I couldn't tell. But I knew one thing—something inside me was changing.

On day four, a therapist sat down with me. He asked me to draw a timeline of my life. I began with the joy of Nasiya's birth, then the pain of James losing his job, followed by the illnesses of my mother and grandmother. I drew a steep, dark descent into hopelessness and fear. Then he asked me to draw what I wanted life to look like.

I sketched a picture of my family—me, James, Nasiya, and Alexis—smiling, hand in hand, full of life. I looked at the drawing and cried. That's what I wanted. That's what I was fighting for.

The next day, I was discharged. The doctors said I was stable enough to return home. My anxiety was still present, but manageable. My depression hadn't disappeared, but I had tools now. I had hope.

James brought Nasiya to pick me up, and when I saw her, I collapsed into tears. I held her like I never wanted to let go again. It was a fresh start.

Before I left, the therapist discussed my aftercare plan, and a nurse handed me my prescription. This time, I wouldn't flush the pills. I knew better. I needed this.

Being back home felt strange. Like stepping into a life I had watched from the outside. I had to relearn how to function as a wife and mother—with the understanding that it was okay to need help. The anxiety lingered, especially my obsessive thoughts about aging. I quoted 2 Corinthians 10:4-5 over and over, trying to cast down every thought. But they still crept in.

At night, I only watched Christian programming. I was afraid of anything else triggering me. I dove into church, showing up to every service, volunteering as often as I could. Maybe if I immersed myself in God's house, I could drown out the fear.

A week after returning home, I started therapy with a Christian counselor. I told her, "I don't feel like God loves me. Why would He let me go through this?"

She listened with compassion. Then she encouraged me to meditate on scriptures about God's love:

> "Dear friends, let us love one another, for love comes from God…" — 1 JOHN 4:7–8
>
> "There is no fear in love. But perfect love drives out fear…" — 1 John 4:18

She helped me face my fear of aging. When I admitted that seeing elderly people made me anxious, she didn't judge me. Instead, she smiled and said, "Write down the blessings of growing older."

So, I did:

- Having grandchildren
- Becoming closer to God
- You don't get older—you get better

- You can do more than you could when you were younger
- Discounts everywhere
- Earning more respect
- Retiring and taking vacations
- Wisdom
- Watching your children succeed
- More time to enjoy your life

Looking at that list gave me peace. For the first time, I saw aging not as a curse but as a gift.

I confessed to my counselor that I had flushed my medication in the past. I was so ashamed. I had even called the doctor's office in tears to admit what I did so I could get a refill. To my surprise, they didn't scold me. They simply helped me.

My counselor said something that stuck with me: "Taking medication doesn't mean God won't heal you."

That truth set me free. So many people—especially in Christian circles—had told me that medication showed a lack of faith. But what about the believers who take insulin or blood pressure medicine? Why is mental health any different?

For the first time, I let go of the guilt. I embraced the help God had provided.

Hope was returning. I knew healing wouldn't come overnight. But I was finally walking toward it.

One step at a time.

Chapter 7

The Struggle is Real

Fear not for I am with you; be not dismayed,
For I am your God. I will strengthen you,
Yes, I will help you,
I will uphold you with My righteous right hand.
— Isaiah 41:10

My Christian counselor suggested I begin journaling to track how I was feeling each day. She explained that documenting my highs and lows would help me identify patterns and monitor my healing. Some days were good, others not so much—but I did what she said.

By May of 2006, I had been on medication for about a month. I still struggled with anxiety and didn't feel quite like myself, but journaling gave me something tangible to focus on. I began recording entries throughout the day—tracking my thoughts, routines, prayers, and progress.

Journal Entry – May 31, 2006

4:08 PM: I'm feeling a little anxiety right now, but I don't want to take my anxiety pill because I know it will make me sleepy. I think the anxiety is tied to my fear of getting older. I'm trying to speak life over this fear:

Older people have more benefits!

I will get better!

I will gain more wisdom!

I will see my kids grow up and get married!

My life will be renewed!

I'll enjoy retirement and grandkids!

4:47 PM: Alexis came home from school, and a wave of fear came over me. I turned on Rod Parsley's sermon, and it calmed me down.

5:17 PM: Anxiety flared up again—same fear of aging. It might have been triggered by the baby crying. I cast the fear away and tried to speak positive words over my mind.

My counselor had told me to meditate on **2 Corinthians 10:4–5**, reminding me to "take every thought captive."

I clung to **1 Timothy 1:7**: *"God has not given me a spirit of fear, but of power, love, and a sound mind."* Some days, I said that verse ten times or more.

6:00 PM: I took my Lexapro and went to church. I felt good being there. It's like, when I'm not consumed with negative thoughts, I feel... normal. But I've gotten so used to thinking the same fearful thoughts over and over that when I go even an hour without them, it feels strange.

10:35 PM: I'm home now, reading before bed. I'm sleepy, so I'm skipping the anxiety pill tonight and trusting God to help me sleep. Stepping out on faith. Good night.

JOURNAL ENTRY – JUNE 1, 2006

4:30 AM: I woke up and couldn't go back to sleep. I went into another room and prayed. I felt some anxiety and intrusive thoughts but cast them out. I went downstairs and turned on Joyce Meyer. I didn't want to lie in bed where the enemy could attack my mind.

As I prayed, I felt the Holy Spirit reveal something: the enemy was using my daughter, **Nasiya**, to deceive me—trying to make me associate her with my fear of aging. That thought broke my heart.

8:30 AM: James, **Nasiya**, and I went walking at the park. I still had to rebuke thoughts whenever I saw older people, but talking with my husband helped.

Still, I kept wondering: *When will this fear go away? I can't live my whole life afraid of getting older.*

10:45 PM: Took my medicine, said my prayers, read a little, and went to bed. No problems falling asleep tonight.

JOURNAL ENTRY – JUNE 2, 2006

5:30 AM: Woke up and couldn't fall back asleep. I stayed in bed until 6:10 AM, then prayed. I ate breakfast and took vitamins. I had some anxiety, so I took a small piece of my anxiety medication and rebuked the thoughts in Jesus' name.

JOURNAL ENTRY – JUNE 3, 2006

I woke up feeling better today. Less anxiety. I had breakfast, which helped, and I didn't need to take any medication this morning.

I went to **Intercessory Prayer** at 6:00 AM with my daughter and a friend. Afterwards, we visited the park and bought some plants.

The lake was peaceful. The sunshine, the water, it all calmed me.

No anxiety until 5:00 PM. I think it was triggered by not eating lunch.

JOURNAL ENTRY – JUNE 4, 2006

Woke up with mild anxiety, but breakfast helped.

Church today was incredible—I attended all three services. I felt renewed in God's presence.

At home between services, I took a nap, but anxiety woke me up around 3:30 PM. After dinner and medication, I returned to church for the evening service.

Later that night, I found out Alexis had left the house. For a moment, panic crept in, I just didn't want her out in the dark.

Turns out, she had simply gone to the clubhouse. So now we know where she disappears when she needs a break from us.

The more I wrote, the more I began to see patterns. I noticed my anxiety spiked in the mornings and that skipping meals made it worse. Walking consistently seemed to help. I also began to identify my safe spaces:

- **Church**—where I felt most at peace.
- **Nature, especially near water**—calming and grounding.
- **Sunlight**—it had a healing effect on my spirit.

I made it a priority to spend time in those places. I continued watching Joyce Meyer and Creflo Dollar and even started reading Joyce's books: *Battlefield of the Mind* and *In Pursuit of Peace*. I'd sit outside in the sun, soaking in the words and the warmth.

Little by little, I started to feel stronger.

I was tired of being afraid.

I was tired of being stuck.

I was ready to fight.

The journaling, the scriptures, the church, the sun, the walks—they were all part of my battle plan. It wasn't over yet, but I could feel it:

My breakthrough was coming.

Chapter 8

Breaking the Chains

He brought them out of darkness and the shadow of death
And broke their chains in pieces.
— Psalms 107:14

Over a month had passed since I began taking medication, and for the first time, I felt a measure of relief. The anxiety and intrusive thoughts were still there, especially the fear, but I was learning how to manage it. Bit by bit, I was starting to find my footing.

I continued seeing my Christian counselor. I honestly don't know what I would've done without her. She had walked beside me, prayed with me, and equipped me with the tools I needed to navigate the storm. Together, we looked through my journal entries and reflected on how far I had come. It was both humbling and encouraging. Even in my lowest moments, God had been carrying me, whether I realized it or not.

She encouraged me to keep writing. So, I did.

Journal Entry – 6/9/06

I woke up at 5:10 a.m. and went straight into prayer. There wasn't much anxiety this morning, and I only needed to take the Lexapro. I'm starting to feel better, but I still don't feel like *myself.* Honestly, I don't even remember who "myself" used to be. It's been so long.

Later, James asked me to help with some life insurance paperwork. I started feeling anxious as he was asking me questions about how much life insurance; I want our kids to have when we passed away. Just hearing those words "passing away" made my anxiety flare up. I was starting to notice my triggers now. If I heard anything about dying or getting older, that was a trigger. I took a walk to help me calm down and came back. I felt better afterward. I took my Lexapro before dinner and ended the day feeling okay.

JOURNAL ENTRY – 6/11/06

I spent the entire day at church—it helped me get through. I cried during the service. I'm not sure why... maybe because I didn't get the job I applied for at the North Campus. I felt like I had let myself down. My self-esteem isn't what it used to be, and I don't feel as energized or optimistic.

But I reminded myself: **The devil is a liar.**

I *will* come out of this. Stronger than ever.

JOURNAL ENTRY – 6/14/06

Anxiety came again this morning, so I went into my closet and prayed. After a while, I felt better. Alexis was home sick with strep throat, so I took care of her all day.

Later that evening, I took **Nasiya** to church. The service was powerful. For a little while, I forgot about everything that was weighing on me.

JOURNAL ENTRY – 6/16/06

Today felt like a setback. I woke up with intense anxiety. I asked myself, *Am I doing something wrong?* I ate breakfast, then took half of an anxiety pill. I turned on Creflo Dollar, and the message was exactly what I needed—about overcoming fear and panic.

He said fear often stems from the past or fear of the future.

That hit me hard. My fear is definitely rooted in the future. I'm afraid I won't be around long enough to care for **Nasiya**.

As for my past… I've been through an abusive marriage and got a divorce. I've had abortions. But I've already laid those at the feet of Jesus. I know I've been forgiven. I don't believe this is punishment anymore.

Journal Entry – 6/25/06

I woke up feeling nervous. I took a Lexapro, but it didn't seem to help much. I don't like taking it in the morning because it makes me drowsy. I prayed and cast out the fear.

I'm tired of talking about this problem. I'm ready to do something about it. Whatever it takes to be free… I'm willing.

At this point, I realized something important:

Only God can set me free.

Not me. Not the medication. Only Him.

Journal Entry – 6/30/06

Today is our wedding anniversary—and James' birthday. I took a walk this morning and felt okay. I honestly don't know if I had anxiety or not.

Even though I didn't get the other position at the church I had an opportunity to apply for another position. I had an interview with the Pastor's wife today, and it went wonderfully. Afterward, I went home to pack for a trip to Nashville to visit family.

I've had frequent headaches lately—maybe from the medication. I prayed that I'd wake up the next day with no anxiety or nervousness.

JOURNAL ENTRY – 7/1/06

Woke up with a little anxiety. James and I went walking at the park—it helped temporarily. Still, I struggled with fear-based thoughts. I want to face them and be free.

That evening, we attended our family reunion. It was beautiful. It was great to see a lot of my family members. This was the first time some of my family got to see Nasiya. I felt good as I socialized with family members. Anxiety was not present as I mingled with everyone.

I got anxious for a moment looking at old photographs of our ancestors. Seeing anyone old or anything resembling aging was a trigger. There was a video of some of our old ancestors that was hard for me to watch, but I faced my fears and I kept looking. I stayed with the discomfort until it passed.

Maybe the key is acceptance.

I can't change the past.

I can't control the future.

But I can trust God with it.

That last journal entry marked a turning point.

My counseling sessions became less frequent because I was improving. To my surprise, I got the job at the church.

I was both excited and nervous. It had been so long since I'd worked. Leaving Nasiya was the hardest part, but financially, it was necessary.

James' savings and military retirement had carried us, but now it was my turn. The only challenge was the commute. Though we lived near the South Campus in Clayton County, my role was at the North Campus in Duluth—an hour or more in traffic.

The morning of my first day, I didn't feel good about it. I didn't want to leave Nasiya. A panic attack hit—I couldn't breathe. Fear consumed me. James helped calm me down. I took deep breaths, got ready, and played worship music the entire drive.

Once I arrived, something shifted. Being around people, being in a structured routine, it helped. I found my rhythm. I made it through the day.

And just like that—I had taken another step forward.

CHAPTER 9

I'M FINALLY FREE

Whom the Son sets free, he is free indeed.
— JOHN 8:36

Three months into taking the medication, I was feeling great. I had a fulfilling job, a wonderful husband, and two beautiful children. Life felt full again—joyful even. For the first time in a long time, I could breathe without the weight of anxiety pressing on my chest.

I even began to wonder if I still needed the medication. I had never taken anything long-term before postpartum depression, and something in me longed for a more natural route. I remembered a woman at church who once introduced me to herbs. That memory stirred something in me.

I went back to the same herb shop I had visited before, and the owner suggested 5-HTP and NeutroCalm, two herbal supplements to help manage mood and anxiety. I didn't know if they would work, but I was open to trying. I began weaning myself off Lexapro—reducing to 10 mg, then 5 mg. Within five months, I was completely off the medication and using only the herbs.

Truthfully, I couldn't tell if the herbs were making a difference or not, because by then, I was already feeling good. Calm. Clear. Whole. It's possible that the medication had built up enough tolerance in my body to help me feel better. I also believed in God's healing power. Through this storm in my life, the Lord completely changed me and made me a new person.

I continued attending my church's Bible study. It remained a critical source of strength and community. Around August, I even found myself able to watch regular television again—something I hadn't done in months. For so long, all I could handle were sermons or worship music. Now, I felt balanced enough to enjoy simple things again.

Even though I was working for the church, I continued volunteering. I found comfort in being active and connected to the body of Christ. The intrusive thoughts and deep fears that had once dominated my mind began to fade away. I found that when I focused on others' problems, it distracted my mind from my own. For the first time in a long time, I felt peace—not just the absence of anxiety, but the presence of peace.

I stayed on herbal supplements through the end of the year. I felt so good that I would forget to take them, and besides, they were getting expensive. After a while, I decided to let them go too. I was finally free.

We held a dedication ceremony for Nasiya at the church, surrounded by loved ones. My best friend, Catherine, stood proudly as the godmother to both of my girls. James's uncle became Nasiya's godfather. It was a beautiful, sacred moment—a full-circle reminder of all we had been through. At the ceremony, I looked very thin because I had lost a lot of weight from the depression. Even though I was feeling good, I still didn't look like myself. Thankfully, no one said anything. They were more focused on celebrating Nasiya.

Grateful for my healing, I poured myself into service. I was at church nearly every day of the week, except Saturdays. I often came home late to find James and Nasiya already asleep. Thankfully, our babysitter was incredibly patient and understanding. She never minded keeping Nasiya longer when we needed her to.

We eventually moved to Hall County to be closer to the church's North Campus. That meant saying goodbye to our beloved babysitter and searching for a new one. We tried several possibilities from the church, but I was very particular. I didn't just want someone to care for Nasiya's basic needs—I wanted her to be active and learning.

One day, I saw a sign that said "Abeka Learning Christian Childcare." I called, and the woman on the other end explained she ran a Christian preschool out of her basement just one neighborhood over. We visited, and Nasiya loved it. It was a blessing. She began learning to read and write early in a nurturing, faith-based environment. She stayed until it was time to begin Pre-K.

I stayed on staff at the church for about three years, but eventually, something in my spirit felt unsettled. I realized I was constantly working and doing, and in the process, I was neglecting my family. Friends began leaving the church, and I felt increasingly alone. I feared slipping back into depression.

James hadn't said anything, but when I brought it up, he admitted he had felt the same way. I was spiritually dry. I was pouring into everyone else but had stopped being poured into. I prayed, "Lord, is this still where You want me to be?" I didn't want to go back into that dark hole again.

So I resigned from my role at the church. Even though I stepped away from leadership, I no longer felt spiritually fed just attending. Something needed to shift.

James suggested we visit Free Chapel in Gainesville, Georgia. I agreed. As the head of our household, I trusted his leadership.

The church was large, and I wasn't sure I would fit in. But when worship began, everything changed. The presence of God was so powerful. The pastor didn't even preach that day. He said the Holy Spirit was leading the church to just worship.

That's exactly what I needed. No pressure. No expectations. No responsibilities. Just me and God. I dropped to my knees and wept, overwhelmed by gratitude. After several visits, we felt led to join.

We officially joined Free Chapel. I was nervous about how my old church would receive the news, but I shared it respectfully because it felt right.

At Free Chapel, I didn't volunteer. I didn't jump into any ministries. I felt God saying, "Just sit, be still, and listen."

So I did. It felt strange not doing anything, but I knew I needed that season of stillness.

In January, the church began its annual Daniel Fast. I felt drawn to participate. It had been nearly four years since I was delivered from postpartum depression, and I believed this fast would bring clarity about my next assignment.

Near the end of the fast, a guest speaker named Perry Stone came to preach. At the end of his sermon, he dropped a black handkerchief to the floor and said,

"If anyone feels like they're living under a dark cloud, come to the altar."

More than 100 people responded. I was shocked so many others were also struggling.

As I watched, something stirred in me. Then I heard it clearly:

"I want you to help My people get out of darkness."

I froze.

"I want you to help My people get out of darkness."

Was God speaking to me? It felt so strong, unlike anything I'd felt before.

A few days later, a former coworker told me she was studying Professional Counseling at Liberty University. Something lit up in me. Maybe this was what God meant.

But doubt came. I'm too old. I don't have the money. I have a toddler and a teenager. How would I manage school?

Still, I called Liberty. The representative shared that as a veteran, I was eligible for a tuition discount. Then came the second surprise: I qualified for the post-9/11 GI Bill because I had served during the time of the 9/11 attacks. It would pay for my tuition and books. I was stunned.

I applied. I was accepted. Just like that, I was a graduate student in my 40s—a wife, a mother, a woman on a mission.

It wasn't easy. Some classes required 20-page papers. Some nights I stayed up doing homework after everyone else was asleep. I cried many times, feeling overwhelmed. But I kept going.

God opened doors. I was able to do my internship at a psychiatric hospital—the same kind of place where I had once been a patient. Now was that coincidental? I don't think so. I believe it was all in his plan. God led me to be a patient at a psychiatric hospital to now working there as an intern.

At first, I was nervous. Now I was on the other side, helping people. I even told some patients that I had once been where they were. Their faces lit up with hope. I met several patients that were experiencing some of the same things I went through and I was able to relate to them. I knew what a panic attack felt like. I knew when you just want to stay in your room and put the covers over you and not see anyone for days. It was a struggle everyday and I was able to help patients know that it gets better and talk to them about some of the things I did to help me. Mostly walking, prayer, socializing, reading my Bible, talking to my therapist, working puzzles, gardening outside, and just being around nature is what I shared with them that helped.

I completed my internship and graduated with zero debt. No loans. No financial burden.

Paid in full. Praise God!

Six months later, the hospital where I interned offered me a job. I served there eight years, helping others navigate darkness.

Eventually, my season there ended. One day, while helping a patient search for counseling, I came across a Christian counseling center in Winder, GA. They didn't accept the patient's insurance, but I couldn't get the name out of my head.

I looked them up again after work and saw they were hiring. I applied, unsure if it would work out, especially after being turned down by my own church. But they called the next day.

About a week after the interview, they made me an offer. I accepted.

God brought me into my dream job as a Christian counselor.

I had written in my Bible three goals:

1. Graduate with my Master's Degree.
2. Get my LPC.
3. Be a Christian Counselor.

God did it.

Everything I went through! Every low, every tear, every prayer was not wasted.

It was hard. But it was worth it.

God took my pain and gave it purpose.

He gave me beauty for ashes.

He gave me peace after panic.

He gave me hope in place of despair.

And now, I stand here—stronger, wiser, and more grounded than ever before.

Because I know this truth without a doubt:

I was set free—not just to survive…but to truly live.

About the Author

Theresa Thomas is a Licensed Professional Counselor who specializes in depression, anxiety, trauma, and working with women who suffer through postpartum depression. Theresa has been counseling for over 11 years and works as a Christian Counselor at The Abundant Life Institute in Georgia. She has been married for 25 years to

her husband James, and they have two beautiful daughters; Alexis, 32 and Nasiya, 19. Theresa is originally from Nashville, TN but has been residing in Georgia for the past 20 years. She is an Army veteran and served in the military for 11 years.

In this book Theresa is hoping to raise awareness that Postpartum Depression is real and that too many women suffer in silence and alone because they are too scared and ashamed to say anything. Through this book Theresa is hoping to shed light on her personal journey and offer insight into how to overcome it by the grace of God and with hope that they can and will have a better life. Postpartum depression does not discriminate; it can affect anyone, even those who walk closely with the Lord. No woman is exempt from this happening to them. This disorder puts women in a dark place, and they have to struggle to get back to reality. If you are a woman that is pregnant or planning to be pregnant, please read this book. To those males who have women in their lives that they love, this book will be great for you too so you can know and understand what goes on in the lives of women who suffer through this ordeal.

As a Christian woman I struggled with the shame of having to take medication and felt like I was not relying on God for my healing. Through the help of a Christian counselor, I was able to overcome the guilt and shame and took the medicine knowing that my healing comes from the Lord. Don't suffer alone. Do yourself a favor and read this book to give you hope that you are going to make it through Postpartum Depression.

SCAN QR CODE TO LEARN MORE

www.ingramcontent.com/pod-product-compliance
Lightning Source LLC
Chambersburg PA
CBHW071347130626
46556CB00005B/2062